DATE LOANED

TOTALLY STEAK
COOKBOOK

THE
TOTALLY
STEAK
COOKBOOK

By Helene Siegel

Illustrated by Carolyn Vibbert

CELESTIAL ARTS
BERKELEY, CALIFORNIA

The Totally Steak Cookbook is produced by becker&mayer!, Ltd.

Printed in Singapore.

Cover design and illustration: Bob Greisen
Interior design and typesetting: Susan Hernday
Interior illustrations: Carolyn Vibbert

Library of Congress Cataloging-in-Publication Data
Siegel, Helene.
    Totally steak cookbook / by Helene Siegel.
        p.   cm.
    ISBN 0-89087-836-6
    1. Cookery (Beef)   I. Title.
TX749.5.B43S553 1997
641.6'62—dc21   96-12653
                                                       CIP

Celestial Arts Publishing
P.O. Box 7123
Berkeley, CA 94707

Look for all 24 *Totally* books at your local store!

TO TED, MY FAVORITE OMNIVORE

CONTENTS

INTRODUCTION

S teak.
The mere mention of it is bound to get either your mouth watering or your blood boiling. No other food elicits the kind of intense emotional reaction that a sizzling slab of beef does.

Steak has ridden the roller coaster of America's love/hate affair with food—especially fatty foods—with a vengeance. In the last fifty years alone it has gone from being the mainstay of the American diet and the celebratory food par excellence—dad barbecuing a giant porterhouse on the patio was the epitome of the 1950s "good life"—to being viewed as a dangerous substance, feared and reviled by many as the enemy.

During the last ten years, the great American steak dinner has been held responsible for a host of ills, from high cholesterol to the expanding national waistline and overactive toddlers. For a while there it seemed that everything bad could be blamed on a slab of meat.

The good thing about food as fashion though, is that the pendulum swings both ways. And these days, it seems to be swinging toward beef. After all, how could something that tastes and smells so good, and that we crave so intensely, be all that bad?

Now that steak is staging a comeback, I for one, am hoping my fellow Americans don't go overboard. When the mood strikes, why not buy a terrific cut of meat, consider the right way to prepare it, cook it to perfection—the recipe for "T-bone Steak Smothered in Onions" on page 84 is as good a place as any to start—and savor every bite? Why not eat a great steak once a week or once a month, rather than every day or not at all?

That way, maybe steak can take its rightful place in the pantheon of truly great American ingredients, without disappearing in another ten years like last year's fashion victim.

"However much we may fancy our avocados and Swiss chard, our sprouts and snap beans and sweet potatoes, from a purely nutritional point of view they can't hold a candle to a nice hunk of meat."

—from Elizabeth Rozin's
The Primal Cheeseburger

STEAK SALADS, SOUPS, AND SANDWICHES

STEAK AND MUSHROOM SANDWICH

Seared mushrooms and steak make a terrific, quick winter's sandwich.

> 4 thick slices country, rye, *or* sourdough bread
> mustard for spreading
> ½ tablespoon butter
> 2 teaspoons olive oil
> 6 ounces shiitake caps, thickly sliced
> 1 teaspoon minced garlic
> salt and freshly ground pepper
> 1 (8-ounce) New York strip steak
> 8 sprigs watercress

Toast the bread, spread with mustard, and set aside on serving plates.

Melt the butter with oil in a large cast-iron skillet over high heat. Sauté the mushrooms just until they begin to wilt, about 2 minutes. Add garlic, salt and pepper, and sauté

1 minute longer. Divide mushrooms
and transfer to bottom slice of each
sandwich.

Season the steak all over with salt and
pepper and sear in the same pan over high
heat. Cook 1½ minutes per side to blacken,
then reduce meat to medium, and cook 1 to
2 minutes more per side. Transfer to cutting
board, and cut into ⅛-inch slices across
grain. Divide and arrange meat over mushrooms. Top each with 4 sprigs watercress and
slice of bread. Cut in half and serve.

SERVES 2

Steak: The Word
The word "steak" derives from the Northern
European Anglo-Saxons. The Saxon word "steak"
meant meat on a stick—*the original method for*
beef barbecue.

PHILLY CHEESE STEAK SANDWICH

Short-order specialties like this never taste quite as good at home, but just in case you can't get out to a greasy spoon, here is the Philadelphia favorite, slightly upgraded in the beef department. If you can find ⅛-inch-thick frozen sandwich or breakfast steaks at the market, by all means substitute the cheaper cut.

4 soft French or Italian rolls, about 8 inches
butter for spreading
1 tablespoon butter
1 tablespoon vegetable oil
2 onions, sliced
¾ pound flank *or* skirt steak,
    frozen 30 minutes and then thinly sliced
salt, freshly ground pepper, and
    garlic powder
Worcestershire sauce to taste
1 cup shredded Monterey Jack *or*
    provolone cheese

Preheat the oven to 400 degrees F. Split the rolls, spread both sides with butter, and place on baking sheet. Toast in the oven about 5 minutes. Remove, leaving the oven on.

Melt the butter with oil in a large cast-iron skillet over medium-high heat. Fry the onions until edges begin to brown. Then push onions to edges of pan.

Season the meat all over with salt, pepper, and garlic powder, and add to the pan. Stir-fry until meat is done, about 1 minute. Sprinkle with Worcestershire and turn out onto cutting board. With a cleaver, roughly chop. Fill each sandwich with meat and onions, and sprinkle on cheese. Return to the oven and bake, open-face, until cheese melts, about 2 minutes. Close sandwiches, cut in half, and serve with ketchup.

MAKES 4

CARNE ASADA TACOS

If you do fire up the grill, toss on some thickly sliced peppers and onions, and also the tortillas, for additional smoky flavor.

1½ tablespoons lime juice
1½ pounds skirt steak
salt and freshly ground pepper
olive oil
8 to 16 flour *or* corn tortillas, warmed
diced onion, avocado, cilantro, and tomato salsa for garnish

Sprinkle the lime juice over the steaks and season all over with salt and pepper.

Preheat a grill or large cast-iron pan over high heat. Lightly coat the pan with oil. Grill or fry the steaks about 1 minute per side, being careful not to crowd the pan. Transfer to cutting board.

Thinly slice the steak across the grain, and roughly chop. Arrange meat in the center of 2 stacked warm tortillas, with condiments at the table to add as desired.

SERVES 4

A Rose by Any Other Name
Names of beef cuts vary according to region and custom. Here is a quick rundown of interchangeable cuts to add to the confusion.

A RIBEYE is a Delmonico, a Spencer, or a filet.
A TENDERLOIN is a filet mignon, a chateaubriand, tournedos, or a tender.
A BONELESS TOP LOIN is a strip, New York strip, Ambassador, Kansas City strip, club, or hotel.
A BONE-IN TOP LOIN is a club, country club, shell, sirloin strip, or Delmonico.
A FLANK is a London broil.
A ROUND TIP is a breakfast, sandwich, or minute.
A SKIRT is fajitas or carne asada.

SIRLOIN CHEESEBURGER DELUXE

The king of cheeseburgers, from the favorite cut of King Henry VIII of England, who dubbed meat from the top rear quarter "sir loin," good enough to be considered royalty.

1 pound ground sirloin
2 ounces blue cheese, crumbled
¼ cup chopped red onion
1 to 2 jalapeños, seeded and minced
salt and freshly ground pepper
1 tablespoon butter, cut in 4 slices
Worcestershire sauce to taste
toasted hamburger buns
thinly sliced onion, tomato slices,
    or lettuce leaves

Lightly combine beef, blue cheese, onion, and jalapeños. Gently form into patties, and season all over with salt and pepper.

Preheat the grill or place cast-iron skillet over high heat. Grill or fry the burgers until bottoms are charred. Flip, and cook second side until done to taste. Do not press to flatten. Top each with a dab of butter and a few dashes of Worcestershire. Serve hot on buns with accompaniments.

SERVES 4

How to Shop for Steak
When it comes to shopping for great steak, look for Choice-graded meat and buy from a busy, clean butcher shop. Lately some of the supermarket warehouses have been carrying excellent grades of beef, so if your freezer space allows, buy in quantity. The meat should be bright red, without gray or brown spots, and the fat should be creamy white, not yellow. The meat should feel firm when pressed. Choose the package with the latest sell date, since it has spent the least amount of time on the shelf. Vacuum-packed beef has a dark purplish color until the package is opened, when the beef should turn red.

THAI BEEF SALAD

Fans of this restaurant favorite usually like it hot, but you can adjust the chiles in the dressing to suit your taste at home. Spicy or not, it is always delicious.

DRESSING
4 garlic cloves, peeled and crushed
1 to 3 serrano chiles, seeded and roughly chopped
1 tablespoon Thai fish sauce
1 tablespoon brown sugar
2 tablespoons lime juice
1 tablespoon cold water

½ pound sirloin
lime juice for drizzling
1 small head Boston *or* bibb lettuce
2 carrots, shredded
½ small red onion, thinly sliced in rings
¾ cup bean sprouts
1 small cucumber, seeded and julienned
vegetable oil for coating

salt and freshly ground pepper
cilantro leaves for garnish

Combine all of the dressing ingredients in a blender or food processor, and purée.

Drizzle lime juice on steak, and marinate at room temperature 30 minutes.

Wash and dry the lettuce, and break into bite-size pieces. Place in bowl, and add carrots, onion, bean sprouts, and cucumber. Toss with half the dressing.

Lightly coat a cast-iron or grill skillet with oil and place over high heat. Season the steak all over with salt and pepper. Panfry steak 3 minutes per side. Cool slightly, and thinly slice across grain. Cut slices into 1-inch lengths. Spoon remaining dressing over meat, and scatter over salad. Garnish with cilantro and serve.

SERVES 4

SEARED SIRLOIN, BLUE CHEESE, AND WALNUT SALAD

Tangy blue cheese and rich, spiced nuts are a natural complement to beef.

1 tablespoon butter
½ cup walnut pieces
salt
pinch cayenne

DRESSING
1 shallot, chopped
½ teaspoon Dijon mustard
3 tablespoons lemon juice
⅓ cup olive oil
salt and freshly ground pepper

8 cups (½ large head) shredded romaine
   lettuce
4 ounces blue cheese, crumbled
¾ pound top sirloin
olive oil for coating

Melt the butter in a small skillet over low heat. Add walnuts, salt, and cayenne, and sauté until nuts are crisp and fragrant, about 5 minutes. Drain on paper towels.

Whisk together the dressing ingredients. Combine lettuce, blue cheese, and nuts in a large bowl. Pour on the dressing. Toss well, and refrigerate.

Season the steak all over with salt and pepper. Lightly coat a grill pan or heavy skillet with oil and place over high heat. Sear the steak 3 minutes per side and remove to cutting board. Cut into ¼-inch slices, and cut each into 1-inch lengths. Scatter beef over salad and serve.

SERVES 4 TO 6

VIETNAMESE SOUP NOODLES WITH FLANK STEAK

Here is an instant version of the wonderfully rich and complex noodle dish from Vietnam—pho. Don't pass up an opportunity to sample the real, restorative thing if there is a Southeast Asian community nearby.

2 ounces rice noodles *or* vermicelli
2 quarts good-quality chicken stock
4 garlic cloves, crushed and peeled
4 (¼-inch) slices fresh ginger, crushed
2 stalks lemongrass, cut in 2-inch lengths
1 jalapeño, sliced with seeds (optional)
2 tablespoons Thai fish sauce *or* soy sauce
1 teaspoon brown sugar
¾ pound flank steak, sliced paper thin along diagonal
2½ cups bean sprouts
6 basil *or* mint leaves
juice of 1 lime *or* lemon

Place the rice noodles in a bowl. Cover with hot water and let sit for 20 minutes to soften. Drain and roughly cut.

Combine chicken stock, garlic, ginger, lemongrass, jalapeño, fish sauce or soy sauce, and brown sugar in a large pot. Bring to a boil, reduce to a simmer, and cook 30 minutes. Remove garlic, ginger, lemongrass, and jalapeño with slotted spoon.

Add softened rice noodles to pot, and bring to a boil. Stir in beef, and remove from heat. Stir in remaining ingredients, adjust seasonings, and ladle into bowls to serve.

SERVES 4 TO 6

ROQUEFORT STEAK TOASTS

These rich little toasts are a nice way to begin a dinner party.

4 tablespoons butter, softened
6 ounces Roquefort cheese, softened
1 long, white baguette, cut in ½-inch slices
¼ pound beef tenderloin *or*
    1 (4-ounce) filet mignon
freshly ground black pepper

Preheat oven to 400 degrees F.

Mash together the butter and Roquefort in a small bowl. Spread about 1 tablespoonful on each slice of bread.

Slice the beef against the grain, as thinly as possible. Top each bread slice with a slice of beef. Arrange in a single layer on baking sheet. Bake until cheese melts and meat is done, about 10 minutes. Season meat with pepper, and serve.

MAKES ABOUT 20, ENOUGH FOR 6 SERVINGS

SMALL MEALS

UPTOWN CHILI

*With such a good cut of meat, this chili cooks to
tenderness much faster than a typical chili. Ask
your butcher to grind the meat in tiny chunks for
chili, and add beans at your own discretion.
Drained beans can be added for an additional
10 minutes cooking time at the end.*

2 tablespoons vegetable oil
1 onion, chopped
3 garlic cloves, chopped
1 jalapeño, seeded and minced
1 pound top sirloin, chili grind
2 teaspoons chili powder
1 teaspoon salt and freshly ground pepper
1 teaspoon ground cumin
½ teaspoon ground coriander
¼ teaspoon cayenne
1½ cups beer
1½ cups canned chopped tomatoes
2 teaspoons crushed dried oregano
2 tablespoons lime juice

chopped onion, cilantro sprigs, grated
cheddar cheese as optional garnish

Heat the oil in a large cast-iron skillet over
medium-high heat. Sauté the onion, garlic,
and jalapeño until soft. Push to the edges,
and add beef. Sprinkle beef with chili, salt,
pepper, cumin, coriander, and cayenne.
Cook, stirring frequently, until meat is evenly browned.

Stir in beer, tomatoes, and oregano.
Reduce to a simmer, and cook about 30 minutes, until thickened to taste. Adjust seasonings, and stir in lime juice. Serve hot with
garnishes and warm tortillas or crusty bread.

SERVES 4

ORANGE BEEF STICKS

The orange's acidity provides a refreshing counterpoint to beef's richness. I like to serve small strips of beef like this as an appetizer or small dinner with bowls of rice.

1 cup fresh orange juice
1½ tablespoons grated orange zest
2 tablespoons soy sauce
1 tablespoon rice wine vinegar
1 tablespoon brown sugar
2 tablespoons peanut oil
1 pound top sirloin, cut in ¼-inch strips

In a shallow bowl, whisk together orange juice, zest, soy sauce, rice wine vinegar, brown sugar, and peanut oil. Add beef strips. Toss to coat evenly, and marinate for 30 minutes at room temperature.

Thread each beef slice on a skewer, reserving the marinade. Heat a grill pan or broiler at medium-high heat, and lightly coat with peanut oil. Pan-grill or broil the skewers until evenly charred, about 1 minute per side. Transfer to serving tray.

Strain marinade into small pan and bring to a boil. Boil 3 to 5 minutes to make a glaze. Spoon over beef sticks and serve.

SERVES 8 AS APPETIZERS

Making the Grade

All American beef is inspected for safety—a procedure that is paid for by taxes. Grading for quality is a marketing system paid for by manufacturers and is based on taste and texture. The top-quality, or Prime, beef has the highest percentage of marble, or fat, in the meat, and comes from cattle no older than three years. Most Prime beef goes to top restaurants and a few special butchers. The next grade, Choice, has less marbling than Prime and includes a wide range of quality. Most of the meat in a good supermarket is Choice. The third grade that makes it to the supermarket is Select. It costs about one dollar less per pound than Choice, and is leaner, but therefore tougher and less flavorful, than the others.

BEEF SATAY

Be careful not to overdo it with a lime juice marinade, since the acids break down muscle and produce an unpleasant texture if meat is marinated too long.

1 pound flank steak
2 garlic cloves, peeled
¼ cup mint leaves
½ onion, in chunks
¼ cup lime juice
1 tablespoon Thai fish sauce *or* soy sauce
1 tablespoon brown sugar
1 tablespoon vegetable oil
prepared peanut sauce for serving

Thinly slice the steak across the width, along the diagonal. Thread the meat on the skewers, leaving about 1 inch bare on each end. Place in a shallow roasting dish.

Combine the garlic, mint, onion, lime juice, fish or soy sauce, brown sugar, and vegetable oil in a food processor or blender, and purée. Pour over the skewers in a pan, and marinate, turning occasionally, ½ hour at room temperature or 1 hour chilled.

Meanwhile, preheat the broiler or grill.

Shake off excess marinade, and arrange the skewers in a single layer on grill or broiler pan. Cook 2 to 3 minutes, turning frequently. Serve hot with peanut sauce for dipping.

SERVES 6 TO 8

Nutritional Lowdown

Part of beef's primal appeal through the ages has been the health-giving properties of animal protein, which contains the amino acids humans need for growth and body repair. A serving of beef delivers protein and fat, with a strong measure of cholesterol, sodium, and iron. Nothing beats beef for building red blood cells.

JAPANESE STOVETOP DINNER

All of the special ingredients for this interactive dinner for two are available at Asian specialty markets—including beef sliced paper thin and prepackaged. The idea for this fun-filled meal came from Los Angeles chef Mary Sue Milliken.

4 cups water
2 (3-inch) pieces kombu seaweed
1½ cups dried bonito flakes
10 ounces beef sirloin *or* ribeye, sliced paper thin by butcher
6 shiitake mushroom caps, halved
4 scallions, cut in 2-inch lengths on diagonal
1 bunch watercress leaves
½ napa cabbage, cut in 1-inch squares
3 ounces firm tofu, in ½-inch cubes
½ cup bean sprouts
Soy Dipping Sauce, recipe follows

Combine the water and kombu in a pot and bring nearly to a boil. Remove kombu and add bonito flakes. Let stand until flakes settle to bottom. Strain broth into large skillet on stovetop or electric skillet at table.

Bring broth to a simmer. Gathering diners around the skillet, use chopsticks to dip beef, a slice at a time, in broth to cook. Dip in sauce and eat. Place remaining ingredients on platter, and add a handful at a time to broth. Pluck, dip, and eat. When only stock remains, pour into 2 bowls and drink.

SERVES 2

SOY DIPPING SAUCE

¼ cup reserved kombu stock
3 tablespoons soy sauce
2 tablespoons mirin (sweet rice wine)
¼ cup rice wine vinegar

Bring the stock, soy, and mirin to a boil. Transfer to a bowl for dipping, and stir in rice wine vinegar.

MAKES ¾ CUP

MUSTARD FLANK STEAK

The world's fastest marinade for delectable next-day sandwich meat.

3 tablespoons grainy *or* Dijon mustard
1 tablespoon soy sauce
1 tablespoon Worcestershire sauce
1 pound flank steak

Whisk together mustard, soy sauce, and Worcestershire sauce. Place steak in shallow bowl, and rub all over with mustard coating. Marinate at room temperature 1 hour or in the refrigerator as long as 4 hours.

Preheat broiler or grill.

Grill or broil steak 4 minutes per side. Let sit on cutting board 5 minutes, and thinly slice along the diagonal, across the grain. Drizzle on juices from cutting board and serve.

SERVES 4

Cooking Tips

- *Remove steak from the refrigerator 1 hour before cooking to bring it up to room temperature.*
- *Season steak all over with salt and pepper before cooking.*
- *Always preheat the grill, broiler, or pan for frying. The proper initial heat will seal in the meat's juices.*
- *The best way to test for doneness is to make a small cut into the thickest part of the steak (near the bone, if there is one) and look at its color: red for rare, pink for medium-rare, tan or beige for medium-well, and brown for well-done.*
- *Marinating is a good way to help tenderize a tough cut or add flavor to any cut. As a general rule, marinate tough cuts such as flank or chuck for 6 to 24 hours in an acidic mixture to break down membranes, being careful not to overmarinate and turn the texture to mush. Tender cuts from the tenderloin, rib, or short loin can also be marinated for extra flavor, but use acids sparingly and do not soak longer than 2 hours in the refrigerator. It takes about ½ cup marinade for each pound of steak.*

BEEF CARPACCIO

The idea of raw beef takes some getting used to, but if it is elegance you are after, nothing could be simpler and more satisfying than a small meal of beef carpaccio and pencil-thin bread-sticks with a glass of red wine.

6 ounces top sirloin *or* New York strip,
    fat trimmed
1½ teaspoons lemon juice
3 tablespoons best-quality olive oil
1 tablespoon sliced chives
¼ teaspoon cracked pepper
¼ teaspoon coarse salt
2 ounces thinly shaved Parmesan cheese

Place the beef in the freezer for about 30 minutes to firm. Cut across grain into ⅛-inch slices. Arrange on cutting board with plenty of space between each slice, and cover with plastic wrap. Using the flat side of a meat pounder, carefully pound each until paper thin. Arrange in a single layer on 4 serving plates. Cover with plastic, and chill as long as 8 hours.

To serve, whisk together lemon juice, olive oil, chives, pepper, and salt. Scatter Parmesan slivers over meat, spoon on dressing, and serve immediately.

SERVES 4

Love Me Tender
If tenderness is what you crave in a steak, you want to avoid those cuts (the chuck and the round) taken from the front and rear muscles near the legs where frequent movement has toughened them. These cuts have great flavor, but it takes long, slow cooking to tenderize the meat and get that flavor into the broth or stewing juices. For the most tender meat, look for cuts from the top midsection, such as tenderloin, T-bone, porterhouse, top sirloin, and rib eye.

CHINESE BEEF AND LONG BEANS

In this typical Chinese presentation, beef plays second fiddle to green vegetables.

½ pound flank steak, cut into
 1 x ⅛-inch strips
1 tablespoon soy sauce
1 tablespoon rice wine vinegar
1 teaspoon cornstarch

SAUCE
¼ cup beef stock
2 tablespoons soy sauce
2 tablespoons rice wine vinegar
¼ teaspoon sugar
peanut oil for coating
4 scallions, white and green, thickly sliced
1½ tablespoons minced garlic
½ pound Chinese long beans *or* green
 beans, trimmed, cut in 1-inch lengths,
 and blanched 2 minutes

Place the beef in a bowl. Add soy sauce, rice wine vinegar, and cornstarch, and toss to coat evenly. Chill 30 minutes.

Combine sauce ingredients in a bowl, and reserve.

Heat a wok or large skillet over high heat and lightly coat with peanut oil. Stir-fry beef just until it turns brown. Transfer to platter and drain pan of excess liquid.

Add scallions and garlic to pan over high heat. Stir-fry less than 1 minute. Add blanched beans, and stir-fry to coat evenly. Pour in sauce, reduce heat to low, and cover. Simmer about 5 minutes. Return beef and juices to the pan, and cook about 1 minute to heat through. Serve with rice.

SERVES 4

ROPA VIEJA

This old California recipe for the Cuban dish of "old clothes"—beef braised to a melting soft-ness—comes from friend Bill Hornaday.

2 pounds flank steak
6 garlic cloves, crushed and peeled
½ teaspoon black peppercorns
1 teaspoon coarse salt
about 2 cups water
3 tablespoons vegetable oil
1 large onion, sliced
2 poblano chiles, roasted, peeled, seeded, and sliced
chopped fresh cilantro, chopped onion, and lime wedges for garnish
flour tortillas for serving

Place the steak in a heavy, medium pot to fit snugly. Add 4 cloves of the crushed garlic, peppercorns, salt, and enough water to cover. Bring to a simmer, cover, and cook about 1½ hours, until tender. Let cool in the broth. Transfer meat to a cutting board, reserving broth.

Using two forks or your fingertips, shred meat and chop into bite-size pieces. Strain the broth, discarding solids, and wipe the pot clean with paper towels.

In the same pot, heat the oil over medium heat. Sauté onion with remaining garlic until soft. Add chiles, and cook an additional 2 minutes. Stir in the shredded meat for about 1 minute, and pour in a cup of the reserved broth to moisten. Simmer 15 minutes to blend flavors. Serve in bowls with cilantro, onion, and lime for adding at the table and tortillas for wrapping.

SERVES 4

BRAISED FLANK STEAK WITH PEPPERS AND ONION

Try leftovers of this classic, also known as steak pizzaiola, reheated and served on crusty Italian rolls.

2 tablespoons olive oil
1 onion, peeled
coarse salt
1 red bell pepper, cored, seeded, and sliced
1 green bell pepper, cored, seeded, and sliced
1½ pounds flank steak
freshly ground pepper
1 cup canned puréed Italian tomatoes
½ cup water
1 tablespoon dried oregano

Preheat the oven to 350 degrees F.

Heat the oil in a heavy pot over medium-low heat. Cook the onion with salt until it begins to soften. Add the peppers and cook

over medium heat, stirring occasionally, about 8 minutes.

Season the steak all over with salt and
pepper, and score a few times to prevent
curling. Place over the onions and peppers,
and add remaining ingredients. Cover, and
bake 1 hour, turning the meat once. Remove
from oven, uncover, and bake an additional
15 to 25 minutes, until sauce is thickened to
taste.

Lift out meat and cool slightly. Thinly
slice across the grain, and serve with sauce.

SERVES 4

Looking for the Lean
Though all American cattle are now bred for leaner
meat than that on which our ancestors chowed
down, some cuts are by nature less fatty. The lean-
est, coming from the round or loin, are top round,
top loin, top sirloin, tenderloin, bottom round, and
eye round.

ASIAN BEEF AND BROCCOLI

Serve this classic Chinese combination over rice or pan-fried noodles.

¾ pound flank steak, thinly sliced across grain in 1-inch strips
2 tablespoons soy sauce
2 tablespoons dry sherry
1 tablespoon cornstarch
1 large stalk broccoli, cut into florets
2 tablespoons Chinese oyster sauce
1 tablespoon water
¼ teaspoon sugar
3 tablespoons peanut oil
1 tablespoon minced garlic
4 scallions, white and green, chopped

Combine the steak, 1 tablespoon each of soy sauce, sherry, and cornstarch in a bowl. Toss to coat evenly, and marinate in the refrigerator 30 minutes.

Meanwhile, blanch the broccoli in boiling salted water or microwave on high about 1 minute. Drain and reserve.

In a small bowl, mix together the remaining soy sauce and sherry, oyster sauce, water, and sugar.

Heat a wok or large skillet over high heat, and swirl in 2 tablespoons of the oil. Stir-fry the beef until the outside is brown, 2 minutes. Transfer to a platter.

Swirl the remaining spoonful of oil into the wok over high heat. Stir-fry the garlic and scallions less than 1 minute. Add the broccoli and briefly stir-fry. Add the soy sauce mixture and cooked beef. Stir and toss an additional minute or two, just to concentrate the flavors, and serve hot.

SERVES 4

EASY BEEF STROGANOFF

Here is a 1950s standard, reproduced without a nod to the cholesterol police.

1 tablespoon butter
1 pound cremini mushroom caps
1 cup julienned dill pickles,
    with 2 tablespoons juice
1½ cups heavy cream
salt and freshly ground pepper
2 pounds beef tenderloin, cut in ¾-inch
    slices across width
2 tablespoons vegetable oil
1 pound wide egg noodles *or* fettuccine,
    cooked and drained

Melt the butter in a large skillet over medium-high heat. Sauté the mushrooms until golden, about 5 minutes. Add pickles with juice, and cook until juice reduces slightly. Add cream and cook until liquid is reduced by half. Season to taste with salt and pepper.

Meanwhile, cook the beef. Season sparingly with salt and pepper, and press by hand to flatten slightly. Heat the oil in another large skillet over high heat. Cook the beef about 2 minutes per side for medium-rare.

To serve, arrange beef over noodles in a serving bowl. Top with sauce to coat evenly, and serve.

SERVES 6

Aged Beef

Aging is considered a good thing for dead meat. If you find it available at a local market or your butcher is willing to custom age, you may want to pay top dollar for the ultimate beef experience. Most aged meat is sold in steakhouses, where you sometimes see glass refrigeration units proudly displaying hanging sides of beef. To be properly aged, beef must be hung in special temperature- and moisture-controlled lockers for twenty-one days. As the meat hangs, its connective tissue breaks down and moisture evaporates, making the steak more tender, intensifying beef flavor, and also increasing its price.

BEER-BRAISED TRI TIP

This light, golden stew improves with a few days in the refrigerator. Serve over wide egg noodles for a scrumptious family meal.

2 pounds sirloin tri tip
salt and freshly ground pepper
paprika
½ cup all-purpose flour
2 tablespoons vegetable oil
4 garlic cloves, chopped
2 teaspoons chopped fresh ginger
2 onions, thickly sliced
3 carrots, peeled and thickly sliced on
   diagonal
1 (12-ounce) bottle beer
2 tablespoons apple cider vinegar
2 teaspoons brown sugar
2 cups beef stock *or* water
2 bay leaves

Cut the beef into large chunks, about 2 x 2 inches. Season all over with salt, pepper, and paprika. Place the flour in a shallow bowl, add the beef, and toss to coat evenly. Pat to shake off excess flour.

Heat the oil in a heavy pot over high heat. Sear the beef on all sides, and transfer to a plate. Reduce the heat to moderate.

Sauté the garlic, ginger, onions, and carrots until golden. Add the beer, vinegar, and brown sugar, and bring to a boil. Cook about 5 minutes. Pour in stock or water, bay leaves, salt, pepper, and seared beef. Bring to a simmer, cover, and cook 1½ to 2 hours, until beef falls off a fork. Serve over hot, boiled noodles.

SERVES 4

ROSEMARY BEEF SKEWERS

Grilled or broiled skewers of meat with vegetables are a sure bet for summer entertaining.

½ cup olive oil
2 teaspoons chopped fresh rosemary
2 tablespoons garlic
salt and freshly ground pepper
1 pound (1-inch thick) sirloin steak, cut into 1-inch cubes
2 onions, in chunks
1 red bell pepper, cored, seeded, and cut in 1-inch squares
1 green bell pepper, cored, seeded, and cut in 1-inch squares
olive oil for brushing
salt and freshly ground pepper

Whisk together olive oil, rosemary, garlic, salt, and pepper. Pour over beef cubes in a bowl and toss to coat evenly. Marinate at room temperature 30 minutes.

Preheat the grill or broiler.

Thread the marinated beef, peppers, and onions on 8 skewers. Brush all over with oil, and season with salt and pepper. Grill or broil about 7 minutes, turning frequently, and serve.

MAKES 8, SERVES 4 TO 8

Steak Storage
Refrigerate meat in its original wrapping up to four days (or one week for vacuum-packed), and place it in the freezer for longer storage. If freezing beef for longer than two weeks, you may want to double-wrap it in freezer paper or storage bags to avoid freezer burn. Defrost in the refrigerator or the microwave, being careful to avoid browning.

CHICKEN-FRIED STEAK

This is a simplified and lightened version of the Texas favorite—more like a breaded veal cutlet than the tougher-than-nails classic—usually served with a heap of gravy and mashed potatoes.

½ cup all-purpose flour
1 teaspoon salt
1 teaspoon paprika
½ teaspoon cayenne
freshly ground black pepper
2 eggs, beaten in shallow bowl
2 cups fine dry bread crumbs
1 pound top round, cut into 4 (½-inch thick) steaks
vegetable oil for frying
lemon wedges and ketchup

Mix together the flour, salt, paprika, cayenne, and pepper on a plate. Nearby, arrange the eggs in a shallow bowl and the bread crumbs in another bowl.

Dip each steak into flour mixture, and transfer to work counter. Pound each side with a flat meat pounder. Then dip each first in the eggs and then in bread crumbs to coat evenly.

Meanwhile, pour the oil into cast-iron skillet to a depth of ½ inch. Heat over high heat. Add the steaks in a single layer, and fry about 1 minute per side to crisp. Reduce heat to medium-low, and continue cooking about 3 minutes per side. Drain on paper towels. Serve hot with lemon wedge and ketchup or condiments of your choice.

SERVES 4

"Texans come out of the womb knowing that they have a special relationship with chicken-fried steak, a divine dispensation granted no one else, and they keep quiet about it for the same reason that a pretty girl doesn't gloat to a plain one."

—from Cheryl Alters and Bill Jamison's
Texas Home Cooking

FAJITAS

Fajitas are a standard weeknight crowd pleaser.

1 pound skirt steak, cut across grain into
   ¼-inch strips
¼ cup lime juice
3 tablespoons olive oil
2 garlic cloves, chopped
1 tablespoon dried oregano, crumbled
½ teaspoon salt
¼ teaspoon cracked black pepper
2 onions, sliced
1 green bell pepper, cored, seeded,
   and sliced
1 red bell pepper, cored, seeded, and sliced
1 jalapeño, seeded and minced
flour tortillas, warmed
assorted salsas and guacamole *or* chopped
   avocado as garnish

Place the steak in a plastic bag. Whisk together the lime juice, 2 tablespoons of olive oil, garlic, oregano, salt, and pepper. Pour over the steak, seal bag, and marinate 1 hour at room temperature or up to 24 hours in the refrigerator.

To cook, drain the meat of the marinade. Heat a large cast-iron skillet over high heat, and add the beef. Stir-fry until just charred, and transfer to a platter. (If beef gives off too much liquid, pour some off so only a spoonful remains in the pan.)

Add the remaining tablespoon of oil to hot pan, and add remaining ingredients. Stir-fry until onions and peppers are browned on edges and beginning to soften. Return beef to the pan and cook briefly just to combine. Serve on platter with warm tortillas, salsas, and guacamole or avocado.

SERVES 4

SAUCES
AND
MARINADES

GORGONZOLA SAUCE

Gorgonzola, Roquefort, Stilton, and blue cheese can be used interchangeably in this rich sauce for your best grilled steaks.

4 tablespoons butter
½ cup diced shallots *or* onion
½ cup port *or* Madeira
1 cup beef *or* chicken stock
4 ounces room-temperature Gorgonzola, crumbled

Melt 2 tablespoons of the butter in a medium skillet or saucepan over medium heat. Sauté the shallots until golden.

Add port or Madeira, and boil until reduced by half. Pour in beef stock and boil until reduced by half again. Reduce heat to low. Whisk in remaining butter, a piece at a time, until smooth. Remove from heat, and whisk in cheese until smooth. Serve immediately over broiled, grilled, or roasted steaks.

ENOUGH FOR 4–6 SERVINGS

FOOD PROCESSOR
BÉARNAISE SAUCE

Here, the classic sauce for filet mignon or any tenderloin cut is made in the food processor.

½ cup red wine vinegar
3 shallots, minced
3 egg yolks
salt and freshly ground pepper
1½ sticks butter, melted and hot
1 tablespoon chopped fresh tarragon
1 tablespoon lemon juice

Combine the red wine vinegar and shallots in a small saucepan. Bring to a boil and cook until a thin film of liquid remains. Strain the reduced vinegar into a food processor fitted with the metal blade. Cool slightly.

Add the egg yolks, salt, and pepper, and process briefly to combine. With the machine on, slowly drizzle in the hot butter. Transfer to a bowl, stir in the tarragon, lemon juice, and salt and pepper to taste.

Serve with grilled, panfried, or broiled filet mignon or sirloin.

MAKES ¾ CUP, ENOUGH FOR 4

Beef and the American Way
Though cattle were first domesticated by the Egyptians in 3500 B.C., it took the vast grazing lands of the New World to make beef available to the masses. Other cultures had domesticated smaller animals as more efficient sources of protein: pigs in China, turkeys in Mexico and South America, sheep in the Middle East, and chickens in India—but no one had tackled the much larger cow. Once Columbus discovered North America and settlers came from Western European cultures that prized beef (though it was mostly eaten by the upper classes), the die was cast. American beef was to set the worldwide standard for both quality and quantity. Beef remains America's most popular meat.

HORSERADISH CREAM

The easiest sauce in the world for one of the smoothest cuts—tenderloin.

3 tablespoons prepared horseradish
1 cup sour cream

Stir ingredients together in a bowl. Serve with "Roasted Tenderloin with Pan Juices" (see page 74) or "Roasted New York Strip" (see page 86).

ENOUGH FOR 6 SERVINGS

SHALLOT COGNAC BUTTER

I prefer a topping like these caramelized shallots to a more elaborate sauce, so the meat's flavor is more pronounced.

1 tablespoon butter
4 shallots, thinly sliced
2 tablespoons cognac *or* brandy

Melt the butter in a small skillet over medium heat. Sauté the shallots until soft and brown along the edges. Pour in cognac and cook until nearly evaporated, about 1 minute. Serve over hot grilled, broiled, or panfried steaks.

SERVES 2

ROQUEFORT BUTTER

Flavored butters can be made in advance, tucked in the freezer, and pulled out on a moment's notice for impressive summer barbecues.

1 tablespoon chopped fresh basil
1 tablespoon sliced chives
1 stick butter, softened
5 ounces Roquefort cheese, softened
¼ teaspoon freshly ground pepper

Combine all of the ingredients in the bowl of an electric mixer, and beat to combine. Or in a food processor with the metal blade, finely chop the basil and chives. Add the butter and process until smooth. Add cheese and pepper and process until evenly blended.

Transfer to sheet of plastic wrap, and shape butter into log. Wrap tightly and refrigerate at least 2 hours. Soften slightly and cut into tablespoon-size slices. Serve on top of hot grilled rib eyes, New York strips, or T-bone steaks.

ENOUGH FOR 8 SERVINGS

GARLIC SALSA FOR STEAKS

The inspiration for this simple vinaigrette comes from the Argentinian restaurant Gaucho Grill in Los Angeles.

½ cup olive oil
¼ cup lemon juice
½ cup chopped fresh Italian parsley
6 garlic cloves, minced
¼ teaspoon red chile pepper flakes
½ teaspoon each salt and freshly
ground pepper

Combine ingredients in a bowl and whisk together. Reserve up to 10 hours in the refrigerator. Spoon over hot grilled or pan-fried steaks.

ENOUGH FOR 8 SERVINGS

FRESH TOMATO SALSA FOR STEAKS

In Latin American countries, where beef is king, a simple fresh salsa of tomatoes is a common accompaniment.

1½ cups chopped plum tomatoes
¼ cup chopped red onion
½ jalapeño, seeded and minced
juice of 1 lime
salt and freshly ground pepper

Mix ingredients together in a bowl. Chill as long as a day. Serve with hot grilled or pan-fried steaks.

ENOUGH FOR 4 SERVINGS

BASIC BEEF MARINADE

*Here is a full-flavored marinade for four
big steaks.*

1 cup olive oil
2 tablespoons dry mustard
1 tablespoon Worcestershire sauce
1 tablespoon minced garlic
1 teaspoon soy sauce
½ teaspoon Tabasco sauce
salt and cracked black pepper

Whisk ingredients together in a bowl and
pour over steaks.

ENOUGH FOR 4 POUNDS OF BEEF

BASIC ASIAN
MARINADE FOR BEEF

½ cup soy sauce
½ cup dry sherry
2 tablespoons grated ginger
2 tablespoons minced garlic
¼ cup sesame oil
2 tablespoons peanut oil

Whisk ingredients together and pour over steak.

MAKES ENOUGH FOR 2 POUNDS OF STEAK

BIG DEALS

HOW TO GRILL A STEAK

Steaks and summer barbecues just seem to have a natural affinity.

any steak except those cut from the round
coarse salt and freshly ground pepper
  to taste
olive oil for rubbing

Remove meat from refrigerator 1 hour before cooking time and season all over with salt and pepper. Rub all over with a light coating of olive oil if not marinated.

Preheat grill very hot.

For thin cuts such as skirt or flank, grill over the hottest spot 2 to 3 minutes per side, and remove. For thicker steaks such as rib eye or porterhouse, start grilling over hottest spot, about 2 minutes per side to sear, then spread out the coals or move to a moderate spot on the grill. Keeping a careful watch, continue cooking, turning frequently, about 5 more minutes per side, or until done to taste. Serve immediately.

HOW TO PANFRY A STEAK

Panfrying in a good, heavy pan like cast-iron is the easiest way to cook a thick, juicy steak to perfection.

filet mignon, rib eye, New York strip, *or* sirloin steak
coarse salt and freshly ground pepper to taste
1 to 2 tablespoons oil *or* half butter and oil

Remove meat from refrigerator 1 hour before cooking time and season all over with salt and pepper.

Heat the pan over high heat for 1 minute. Add the oil or butter-and-oil mixture, and heat for a moment. Add steaks, being careful not to crowd the pan, and cook until seared on both sides, about 2 minutes each side. Then reduce the heat to medium and cook 3 to 5 minutes per side, until done to taste. Let sit 5 minutes and serve.

HOW TO BROIL A STEAK

Since so little control is possible, the best steaks for broiling are no more than ¾ inch thick, so that once the outside is seared, the inside is more or less cooked also.

flank, rib eye, sirloin, T-bone, *or* porterhouse steaks
coarse salt and freshly ground pepper to
taste

Remove meat from refrigerator 1 hour before cooking time, and season all over with salt and pepper.

Preheat the broiler for 15 minutes. Arrange rack about 4 inches from heat and line tray with foil for easy cleanup.

Place meat on broiler tray, and cook until top is evenly charred, no longer than 5 minutes per side. Flip over and broil until second side is evenly cooked. Transfer to cutting board and let rest 5 minutes for steaks that need slicing.

TUSCAN-STYLE GRILLED STEAK

The Italian style is simplicity itself—a good piece of meat perfectly grilled and then dressed with a dash of olive oil, salt, and pepper. Serve with other simple foods such as roasted potatoes, grilled vegetables, and some good crusty bread.

porterhouse *or* T-bone steaks
coarse salt and freshly ground pepper
good-quality olive oil for drizzling
lemon wedges

Remove steaks from refrigerator 1 hour before cooking. Preheat the broiler or prepare the grill.

Season the steaks all over with salt and pepper. Broil or grill over highest heat, about 2 minutes per side for medium-rare. Transfer to serving platter, lightly drizzle with oil, and serve with salt, pepper, and lemon wedges.

ROASTED TENDERLOIN WITH PAN JUICES

Cooking a whole tenderloin and then slicing it into steaks is an easy way to serve an impressive dinner for a group. If making in advance, cut steaks after reheating.

1 (2-pound) beef tenderloin
coarse salt and cracked pepper
¼ cup beef stock *or* water
4 tablespoons butter
¼ teaspoon red currant *or*
    grape jelly (optional)

Preheat oven to 450 degrees F.

Season the meat all over with salt and pepper, and place in roasting pan. Roast, uncovered, 30 minutes for medium-rare. Transfer to cutting board, and cool 5 minutes.

Cut the beef into ½-inch slices across the grain, and arrange on platter. Keep warm in 200-degree oven.

Pour the juices from the board back into the roasting pan, and place on stovetop. Add stock or water and butter to pan, and place over high heat. Bring to a boil, scraping the bottom to release any browned bits. Whisk in optional jelly, and remove from heat. Pour into sauceboat to pass at table.

SERVES 4 TO 6

FILET MIGNON TEXAS STYLE

Top these spice-rubbed beauties with a cool,
fresh citrusy salsa like mango or pineapple and
serve with corn on the cob, for a real Texas treat.

1 tablespoon paprika
2 teaspoons chili powder
½ teaspoon onion powder
½ teaspoon ground cumin
½ teaspoon salt
½ teaspoon sugar
½ teaspoon freshly ground black pepper
¼ teaspoon dry mustard
¼ teaspoon cayenne pepper
¼ teaspoon curry powder
¼ teaspoon ground coriander
4 (4- to 6-ounce) filet mignons
2 tablespoons vegetable oil

Mix the spices together in a small bowl. Generously season the filets by rubbing and patting all over with spice mix. Let sit at room temperature 1 hour.

To cook, heat the oil in a large, heavy skillet over medium-high heat. Fry the steaks 3 minutes per side for medium-rare. (Do not worry about blackened crust.) Serve immediately.

SERVES 4

"More than fish, shellfish, or poultry, mammal flesh provides a high percentage of fat, some of which surrounds the muscle tissue and some of which is marbleized within it. And it is this rich protein-fat package that is of such compelling appeal to the human consumer."
　　　　—from Elizabeth Rozin's
　　　　The Primal Cheeseburger

STEAK AU POIVRE

Fragrant black pepper is a terrific match for the richness of beef in this French classic.

2 (8- to 10-ounce) rib eye, sirloin, *or*
    Spencer steaks
salt
4 teaspoons cracked black peppercorns
1 teaspoon vegetable oil
2 tablespoons plus 1 teaspoon butter
2 tablespoons cognac *or* brandy
½ cup beef *or* chicken stock

Season the steaks all over with salt, and divide pepper into 4 portions. Press each portion onto each side of steak, and let sit ½ hour at room temperature.

Heat the oil with 1 teaspoon of butter in a large skillet over high heat. Cook the steaks 4 minutes per side for rare. Transfer to serving plates.

Remove pan from heat, swirl in the cognac or brandy, and return to high heat. Pour in the stock and boil about 4 minutes. Remove from heat, and stir in 2 tablespoons of butter, a small piece at a time, until sauce is smooth. Pour over the steaks, and serve.

SERVES 2

TENDERLOIN WITH TOMATOES AND BASIL

In this quick summertime dish fresh tomatoes and basil transform a rich cut of beef into a light, refreshing, well-balanced meal.

1 pound beef tenderloin
¼ cup olive oil
2 tablespoons water
1 bunch fresh basil leaves, thinly sliced
6 garlic cloves, minced
2 plum tomatoes, seeded and sliced

Cut the beef against the grain into ¼-inch slices. Pound to ⅛ inch and reserve.

Heat the oil and water in large skillet over medium-high heat. Cook the basil, garlic, and tomato until the basil wilts, about 4 minutes. Add the beef slices, and sauté briefly, about 1 minute per side. Season to taste with salt and pepper, and serve immediately.

SERVES 4 TO 6

JALAPENO FLANK STEAK

Chile pepper lovers will not be disappointed in this zesty marinade—not for the faint of heart.

3 jalapeño peppers
4 garlic cloves, peeled
½ tablespoon cracked black pepper
1 tablespoon coarse salt
¼ cup lime juice
1 tablespoon dried oregano
½ cup olive oil

Combine the jalapeños, garlic, black pepper, salt, lime juice, oregano, and oil in a food processor or blender, and purée. Pour over meat in shallow roasting pan and evenly coat. Cover and marinate in refrigerator 2 to 24 hours.

Preheat grill or broiler.

Grill or broil 5 minutes per side for medium-rare. Let sit 5 minutes before slicing. Cut into thin slices across the grain and serve hot.

SERVES 4

GARLIC-STUDDED RIB EYE

A well-marbled steak like ribeye stands up well to the assertive flavor of garlic.

12 garlic cloves, unpeeled
4 (1-inch-thick, 10-ounce) ribeye steaks
salt and freshly ground pepper
olive oil
lime wedges for garnish

Place the garlic cloves in a small, dry skillet over high heat. Cook, turning occasionally and pressing down with tongs to blacken evenly, about 7 minutes. Let cool. Peel and cut large cloves into thick slivers, leaving small cloves whole.

With a sharp paring knife, make several slits in each steak along the natural breaks. Stuff each with a garlic sliver, and season the steaks generously with salt and pepper.

Preheat the grill or heat a large skillet over high heat. Lightly coat the skillet with oil. Grill or sauté the steaks 3 to 4 minutes per side for medium-rare. Serve hot with lime wedges.

SERVES 4

T-BONE STEAK
SMOTHERED IN ONIONS

In this panfried favorite, chunks of caramelized onion and wedges of sweet tomato contrast and enhance steaks to perfection.

2 (8- to 10-ounce) T-bone steaks
1 large garlic clove, crushed
salt and freshly ground pepper
1 tablespoon olive oil
1 large onion, cut in 8 wedges
2 teaspoons minced garlic
½ jalapeño pepper, seeded and minced
2 plum tomatoes, cut in 8 wedges
    lengthwise
2 teaspoons butter

Remove steaks from refrigerator 1 hour in advance. Rub all over with crushed garlic, season with salt and pepper, and let sit.

Heat the oil in a large cast-iron skillet over high heat. Panfry the steaks about 2 minutes per side. Transfer to a platter.

Reduce the heat under pan to medium. Sauté onion until golden along edges but still firm. Increase heat to high, and add garlic and jalapeño. Cook, stirring frequently, less than 1 minute. Add tomatoes, salt, and pepper, and continue cooking over moderate heat, stirring frequently, until onion begins to caramelize and tomatoes soften, 5 to 8 minutes. Add steaks with accumulated juices and butter to pan. Stir and toss just to heat through. Serve steaks smothered with sauce.

SERVES 2

ROASTED NEW YORK STRIP

I find it much less daunting to serve a crowd excellent meat simply roasted than to cook each steak to order. Increase cooking time about 12 minutes per pound for a larger piece, and accompany with potatoes—mashed, french fries, or pancakes are all delightful choices.

1 (2-pound) New York strip *or* loin strip
salt and freshly ground pepper
olive oil for coating

Preheat the oven to 425 degrees F. Season the meat all over with salt and pepper.

Heat a cast-iron grill pan or skillet over high heat. Coat the pan with oil and add the beef. Sear (fat-side first) until browned, about 2 minutes per side. Transfer to the oven and roast, uncovered, about 35 minutes for rare. Turn once at about 15 minutes.

Let sit on cutting board 5 minutes. Cut across width into 4 slices, and serve.

SERVES 4

A Few Choice Cuts

TENDERLOIN is the long thin muscle that runs under the short loin, behind the ribs. From the tenderloin, which is one of the most expensive cuts, four different steaks can be cut. All are prized for their tenderness more than for their flavor, and they are often matched with strong sauces like béarnaise to make up for that lack. "Buttery-soft" is an apt description of a tenderloin steak. The first or thickest cut is a chateaubriand, a double-thick steak for two, named for a statesman from the Napoleonic era, who must have been known for his largesse. Next are filet steaks, followed by tournedos, and at the narrow end, filet mignon, a short, thick slice of perfection. At the very end the tenderloin comes to a tip, from which strips can be cut for dishes such as Stroganoff. The tenderloin can be roasted whole (see page 74) or steaks can be panfried for best results.

PLUM GINGER STEAK

Chinese plum sauce, a sweet gingery chutney available in jars in Chinese markets, is a nice, easy counterpoint to ginger-marinated steaks. For a delightful special dinner, serve with seared spinach or Chinese broccoli and rice.

¼ cup soy sauce
¼ cup dry sherry *or* rice wine
2 tablespoons honey
¼ cup minced ginger
2 (6- to 8-ounce) New York strip steaks
prepared Chinese plum sauce

In a shallow nonreactive pan (large enough to hold steaks), whisk together soy, sherry or wine, honey, and ginger. Add steaks, turn to coat evenly, and marinate 1 hour at room temperature or 3 hours in the refrigerator.

Preheat grill or broiler.

Grill or broil over high heat about 3 minutes per side for rare. Transfer to serving plates and spread about 1 tablespoonful of plum sauce over each steak. Serve hot.

SERVES 2

A Few Choice Cuts

PORTERHOUSE or T-BONE steaks are cut from the short loin. They have the bone left in, with a well-marbled strip steak on one side and a tender filet portion on the other. They are a great choice for those who crave variety and a good bone to gnaw. The porterhouse is larger than the T-bone, and both cuts take well to high-heat methods like grilling, broiling, or panfrying.

FLANK STEAK—the lean, flat, boneless muscle with long, coarse grains that runs along the cow's underside—is the most versatile cut. It is delicious seasoned and broiled for London broil (the dish, not the cut), marinated and grilled, cut into strips and stir-fried, braised in liquid, and even stuffed and rolled. Since it is moderately priced and so easy to cook, it fits in well with family cooking. Leftover slices make terrific steak sandwiches.

TEQUILA PEPPER STEAKS

Substitute port, Madeira, or your favoite fortified wine for the tequila for a delicious, lightened wine sauce for beef.

2 (6- to 8-ounce) New York strips *or*
     Spencer steaks
salt and cracked black pepper
1 tablespoon peanut *or* vegetable oil
¼ cup tequila
½ cup dry white wine
½ cup beef *or* chicken stock
1 tablespoon butter

Season the steaks all over with salt and cracked pepper.

Heat the oil in a large skillet over medium-high heat. Panfry the steaks about 4 minutes per side for medium-rare. Remove steaks to plates.

Drain the pan, and add tequila off the heat. Return pan to medium heat, and cook until 1 or 2 teaspoonfuls of tequila remain.

Pour in wine, and boil until reduced by half. Pour in beef stock, and cook until reduced again by half. Remove from heat, and stir in butter until smooth. Spoon sauce over steaks and serve.

SERVES 2

A Few Choice Cuts

HANGER STEAK, also known as onglet by the French, is a ½-inch-thick, long, narrow muscle that hangs under the tenderloin. Because of its odd size and its singularity (each cow has just one), this well-marbled, flavorful, grainy cut was usually brought home and eaten by the butcher's family. But now it is gathering a following among beef lovers. Onglet has long been prized by the French, who serve it in bistros with their de rigueur pommes frites. It's not available at supermarkets, but you may be able to order it from a butcher, who would probably recommend panfrying or grilling it medium-rare.

STUFFED FLANK STEAK WITH WILD MUSHROOMS

*Look for the biggest piece of flank for easier but-
terflying—or ask the butcher to cut it for you.
Flank steak takes beautifully to this type of slow-
braised soulful cooking. Mashed potatoes are the
perfect accompaniment.*

1 (1½- to 2-pound) flank steak
salt and freshly ground pepper
4 tablespoons butter
½ onion, chopped
8 ounces brown cremini mushrooms,
  cleaned and roughly chopped
4 ounces shiitake mushroom caps, cleaned
  and roughly chopped
3 garlic cloves, minced
1 tablespoon cognac *or* brandy
¼ cup milk
2 slices white bread, crusts removed
  and cubed
½ beaten egg

2 tablespoons chopped fresh
   Italian parsley
1 tablespoon vegetable oil
2 cups beef broth
1 cup white wine

Butterfly the flank steak by slicing it horizontally, leaving one edge attached. Lay open and season all over with salt and pepper.

To make the stuffing, melt 3 tablespoons of the butter in a large skillet over medium heat. Cook the onion until soft. Add all the mushrooms, turn the heat to high, and sauté until the liquid is released. Add garlic, salt, and pepper and cook less than 1 minute. Pour in cognac or brandy, and cook until liquid is nearly all absorbed. Remove from heat.

In a large mixing bowl, combine milk and bread cubes and evenly moisten. Add mushroom mixture, egg, and parsley, and mix well.

Preheat oven to 350 degrees F.

Spread the stuffing in an even layer all over opened steak. Roll, jelly-roll fashion, and tie with string or fasten with toothpicks to enclose.

Melt the remaining butter and oil in a flameproof roasting pan over high heat. Add rolled meat, and sear all over. Pour in the beef broth and wine. Cover and bake 1½ hours, until meat falls off a fork. Set aside to cool on a board.

Meanwhile, strain the liquid from the roasting pan into a smaller pan. Bring to a boil, and skim and discard fat from top. Boil 3 to 5 minutes, season with salt and pepper, and remove.

To serve, remove the strings or toothpicks from the steak. Carefully cut across the width into ½-inch slices. Arrange on platter, and spoon on hot pan juices. Serve immediately with mashed potatoes.

SERVES 6 TO 8

Mail-order Steaks

BOYLE MEAT COMPANY
Kansas City, MO
(800) 821-3626

BURGER'S MEATHOUSE
California, MO
(800) 624-5426

CLASSIC STEAKS
Omaha, NE
(800) 288-2783

GOLDEN TROPHY STEAKS
Chicago, IL
(708) 517-9144

HARRY AND DAVID
Medford, OR
(800) 547-3033

OMAHA STEAKS
Omaha, NE
(800) 228-9055

PFAELZER BROTHERS
Burr Ridge, IL
(800) 621-0226

SMITHFIELD COLLECTION
Smithville, VA
(800) 628-2242

STEW LEONARD'S
Norwalk, CT
(800) 729-7839

CONVERSIONS

LIQUID
1 Tbsp = 15 ml
½ cup = 4 fl oz = 125 ml
1 cup = 8 fl oz = 250 ml

DRY
¼ cup = 4 Tbsp = 2 oz = 60 g
1 cup = ½ pound = 8 oz = 250 g

FLOUR
½ cup = 60 g
1 cup = 4 oz = 125 g

TEMPERATURE
400° F = 200° C = gas mark 6
375° F = 190° C = gas mark 5
350° F = 175° C = gas mark 4

MISCELLANEOUS
2 Tbsp butter = 1 oz = 30 g
1 inch = 2.5 cm
all-purpose flour = plain flour
baking soda = bicarbonate of soda
brown sugar = demerara sugar
heavy cream = double cream
sugar = caster sugar